P9-CFB-371

DISCARD

Sophisticated Ladies

THE GREAT WOMEN OF JAZZ

LESLIE GOURSE · ILLUSTRATED BY MARTIN FRENCH

DUTTON CHILDREN'S BOOKS

This book is dedicated to the talented new generation of jazz singers, men and women, who have learned their craft and try to maintain the high standards of the classic singers. Among the great or at least fascinating newcomers are Dee Dee Bridgewater, Patricia Barber, Harry Connick Jr., Carla Cook, Dena DeRose, Kurt Elling, Nnenna Freelon, Giacomo Gates, Al Jarreau, Bobby McFerrin, Norah Jones, Susannah McCorkle, John Pizzarelli Jr., Kevin Mahogany, Kendra Shank, Lea DeLaria, and Jeffery Smith.

—LG

For Kristi

—MF

DUTTON CHILDREN'S BOOKS
A division of Penguin Young Readers Group

Published by the Penguin Group
Penguin Group (USA) Inc., 375 Hudson Street, New York, New York 10014, U.S.A. • Penguin Group (Canada), 90 Eglinton Avenue East, Suite 700, Toronto, Ontario, Canada M4P 2Y3 (a division of Pearson Penguin Canada Inc.) • Penguin Books Ltd, 80 Strand, London WC2R 0RL, England • Penguin Ireland, 25 St Stephen's Green, Dublin 2, Ireland (a division of Penguin Books Ltd) • Penguin Group (Australia), 250 Camberwell Road, Camberwell, Victoria 3124, Australia (a division of Pearson Australia Group Pty Ltd) • Penguin Books India Pvt Ltd, 11 Community Centre, Panchsheel Park, New Delhi—110 017, India • Penguin Group (NZ), Cnr Airborne and Rosedale Roads, Albany, Auckland 1310, New Zealand (a division of Pearson New Zealand Ltd) • Penguin Books (South Africa) (Pty) Ltd, 24 Sturdee Avenue, Rosebank, Johannesburg 2196, South Africa • Penguin Books Ltd, Registered Offices: 80 Strand, London WC2R 0RL, England

Library of Congress Cataloging-in-Publication Data
Gourse, Leslie.
Sophisticated ladies : the great women of jazz / by Leslie Gourse ; illustrated by Martin French.—1st ed.
p. cm.
Includes bibliographical references (pp.62–63) and discography (pp.63–64).
ISBN: 978-0-525-47198-1
1. Women jazz singers—Biography—Juvenile literature. I. Title.
ML3929.G675 2007 782.42165092'2—dc22 [B]
2006014852

Published in the United States by Dutton Children's Books,
a division of Penguin Young Readers Group
345 Hudson Street, New York, New York 10014
www.penguin.com/youngreaders

Designed by Jason Henry
Manufactured in China • First Edition
1 3 5 7 9 10 8 6 4 2

Contents

Introduction: Bending the Notes

THESE ARE THE STORIES OF FOURTEEN FABULOUS WOMEN, blues and jazz singers all. They helped create, and are, a uniquely American art form that began in the twentieth century and has moved into the twenty-first. Their art came from their backgrounds, which were often rooted in the small poverty-ridden towns of the South. And it came from the ever-changing musical styles of the early twentieth century. They took that culture and, each in her own way, wove it into a personal style. They set new standards for melody, harmony, and rhythm. These women have often been imitated but never equaled. Each is unique. Ella is Ella and Bessie is Bessie, a blend of voice and heart and talent that is like no other.

Their songs are as unique as themselves, romantic and funny, slow and sad, and always real. Many of them learned the melodies as gospel singers in their local churches. Many were band singers in saloons all around the land. They could glide from one note to the next in a technique called "bending the notes." It was an important part of jazz and individual style, known as improvisation.

They may have been special and talented, but this was no pampered group of performers, especially in the early years. In those days, for most of them, getting work meant getting on the road. Traveling in buses from town to town, from honky-tonk saloon to small nightclub, was not only difficult but also often dangerous. They ate when they could find a restaurant and had money. They slept at odd hours. Many used alcohol and drugs to keep themselves awake or get themselves to sleep or to hide the loneliness and fear. All they had to rely on was the voice that could charm an audience or leave it cold. There was little time for a personal life. Those who married or formed relationships with other performers or club managers sometimes found themselves cheated out of their paychecks. All they could do was get on the bus again.

But still they sang. It was what they did, what they were and are. Out of that early gospel music came the blues, those painful, sweet, all-too-real stories of everyday life. It came from the language of the streets set to church music. The blues wailed about faithless lovers, about poverty, homelessness, and lonesomeness—and the good times, too.

The blues came from a relatively simple folk music with a structure. The music borrowed the call-and-answer techniques of gospel. It imitated the back-and-forth sing-speech between minister and audience in church. Blues singers used the same technique to add drama and feelings to their songs. The magic of the blues came from the singer's power to lift her audiences out of their own feelings of sadness and despair.

From the blues came the art of jazz singing. By the 1920s, it was a recognized performing style. All the music of the times was blended into a swinging beat. Improvements in recording techniques allowed singers to reach a wider audience.

All these blues and jazz singers were—and are—masters of a compelling, American kind of music. Here are fourteen fabulous "girl" singers. They have a rare quality beyond their musical ability. In their art, in their lifestyles, they convey a fine sense of experience and worldliness. These women are from different backgrounds, rarely the highest of society. Yet they appeal to everyone. Their art is appreciated by the richest and the poorest. They are the best of the best. They are the sophisticated ladies of jazz.

Bessie Smith

The Blues

CAREER YEARS: 1915–1930s

THE GREATEST CLASSIC BLUES SINGER of the 1920s was a tough-talking, hard-drinking woman from Tennessee named Bessie Smith (1894–1937). She stood six feet tall and never backed down from an argument. But sometimes when she was onstage, such tenderness flowed out of that huge sweeping voice that her audiences cried. Bessie was called the "Empress of the Blues" simply because no one of her time could match her. A bold, confident performer, she wove all the dreams and bitterness of African-Americans into her music.

Bessie was born into poverty and in a sense never left it. Pain and sadness filled her work. She was born in a cabin in Chattanooga, on April 15, probably in 1894, although the date is uncertain. There was little food and never much schooling, but she did learn to read and write. Orphaned at ten, Bessie was raised by her oldest sister, Viola.

She grew into a handsome girl with an exceptionally strong voice, and she sang for money on street corners at night. On one such night around 1912, Ma Rainey and her Rabbit Foot Minstrels came to town in a traveling tent show. Performers set up tents in towns around the South to entertain the local audiences. Rainey, one of the first of the great blues singers, heard Bessie singing on the corner. She took the young girl with her powerful voice on the road, away from Tennessee and her family.

For the next three years, Ma Rainey coaxed Bessie's voice into an instrument that wound around a syllable or gave a line new meaning by a gentle accent. Her voice was so strong that she usually sang without a microphone. And she did not like a drummer setting the tempo. "I set my own beat," Bessie said. The effect on her audiences was mesmerizing.

Bessie left Rainey in 1915 to play in the small theaters and saloons of cities in the South. She became one of the most popular singers in vaudeville and was eventually heard by pianist Clarence Williams, who worked for Columbia Records. He got Bessie her first recording contract in February 1923. The song was "Down Hearted Blues," and it sold two million copies, remarkable for that time. "Trouble, trouble," sang Bessie, "I've known it all my days."

Soon after the recording, Bessie married Jackie Gee, a Philadelphia policeman who came to see her perform. They loved each other and adopted a son, Jackie Jr., but Bessie was always on the road. And she drank too much. A heavy drinker since her teens, she took to downing tumblers of gin—her favorite—before a performance. Sometimes she could not even go onstage. That made her depressed, and it made her mean. Bessie was a fighter when she drank.

Even so, Bessie Smith's short career was amazing. She became the nation's highest-paid black entertainer and one of the biggest stars of the 1920s. Of her many recordings with famous artists, her version of "St. Louis Blues" with Louis Armstrong is regarded by critics as one of the greatest of the decade. Audiences, black and white alike, adored her. Bessie sang of lost love, of poverty, and of the sadness that comes from being black in a white world. She especially sang of lost love in 1930 when she and Jackie separated because their lives were so different.

American music was also changing in the 1930s. Audiences living through the Depression welcomed the lively new sound of swing. So Columbia Records dropped Bessie Smith. Her drinking got worse. Agents were afraid to hire her for fear she would not show up for a performance. And even though she had made so much money, she was back in poverty. Bessie either gave away her money when she had it or spent it foolishly.

In 1936, Bessie Smith made her last public appearance in New York City at the Famous Door. The following year, she was in an automobile accident in Clarksdale, Mississippi. Her right arm was nearly cut off, and she died from loss of blood. Rumors persisted that she died because a nearby hospital would not admit a black person. That was never proven. Playwright Edward Albee wrote about it in his *The Death of Bessie Smith* (1960). Her grave was unmarked until 1970 when singer Janis Joplin and others paid for a headstone.

Bessie Smith won two Grammys and is in the Blues Foundation Hall of Fame (1980). She left behind some 160 recordings, nearly all reissued and most of them blues masterpieces. They bring alive the powerful earthiness, the great strength, and the remarkable tenderness of a voice like no other. It made Bessie Smith "Empress of the Blues."

9

Ethel Waters
Stormy Weather

STORMY WEATHER," SHE SANG, "just can't get my poor self together, keeps rainin' all the time." For Ethel Waters (1896–1977), stormy weather was more than a song. It was forever part of this multitalented woman. Ethel was a fine blues singer, a much-admired Broadway actress, and an Oscar-nominated Hollywood star. She sang blues and jazz with perfect diction even though she had little education and could not read music. One of the most popular and influential of blues singers, she was an innovator. She was a singer who blended the music of blues, jazz, and vaudeville into a sophisticated style that could only have come from Ethel.

Music critics called her voice "sweet" and bell-like, not the usual deep sound of the Southern blues. She sang the way she felt. When she was happy, her audiences smiled with her; when she was sad, they felt her pain.

The pain in Ethel stemmed from her earliest days. She was born in Chester, Pennsylvania, on October 31, 1896, in the most dreadful of circumstances. Her twelve-year-old mother had been sexually assaulted. Ethel was sent to Philadelphia to be raised by her grandmother, who could barely support herself by cleaning houses. As a young teenager, Ethel began to clean houses, too.

Soon she dropped out of school and began working as a hotel maid. She liked to sing and practice in front of the hotel room mirrors. She earned $4.75 a week.

But Ethel got a raise in 1917, when she won an amateur night contest. She began singing at a local club in Baltimore for $9 a week. Before long, people were talking about this slender blues singer whose voice was so different from the traditional deepness of the South. She was known as "Sweet Mama String-bean."

By 1921, Sweet Mama was in New York City, where she first appeared on Broadway in *Africana* and in musical revues. Irving Berlin cast her in his all-white Broadway show *As Thousands Cheer*. Her first recording, for the little-known Black Swan label, was released in 1921, before the great Bessie Smith's first release. Ethel became a favorite on the nightclub scene, making the song "Dinah" a huge hit. But in 1933, she became a hit herself at the Cotton Club in Harlem. It was there that she first sang "Stormy Weather" with Duke Ellington's orchestra. It became her song, a story of all the misery and sadness she had known in her life.

Music lovers began to talk about this young woman with the sophisticated style. More Broadway appearances followed. Theater critic Brooks Atkinson said she "knows how to make a song stand on tiptoe." Ethel also received great praise for dramatic roles, such as the maid in *The Member of the Wedding*. She was the first black woman to get star billing on the American stage.

As successful as she was, in the 1940s Ethel had trouble finding work. She moved to Hollywood and appeared in *Cairo* in 1942 and *Cabin in the Sky*, with Lena Horne and Duke Ellington, in 1943. She returned to New York, but it wasn't always easy for a singer to find work during World War II. But by the end of the decade, her luck changed. Before long she was as successful in the movies as she had been onstage; overall she appeared in ten films. She was nominated for an Academy Award for her role as the maid in *Pinky* (1949), about a black woman living as white in the South. (She lost the supporting Oscar to Mercedes McCambridge for *All the King's Men*.) Ethel did win the New York

Drama Critics Award as best actress, however, in 1950, for her performance in *The Member of the Wedding*. In 1951, she published her autobiography, *His Eye Is on the Sparrow*. The title comes from a gospel song in *The Member of the Wedding*.

By the late 1950s, although successful, Ethel began to question what her career was all about. Always a religious woman, she was moved by the words of evangelist Billy Graham when he spoke at a Madison Square Garden rally in New York City. Ethel joined his crusading organization and, in a singing role, toured with him.

She may have been the first female African-American superstar, but Ethel Waters did not experience much personal happiness in her life. She was married three times; all failed. She constantly fought health problems. A large woman, at one time reaching 350 pounds, she was a diabetic. She was also plagued with money troubles in her later years. Although she earned a million dollars, in 1957 the IRS cited her for not paying taxes. As Ethel said, she never had a "working acquaintance" with wealth and just didn't know how to keep it. She died in 1977 in California at the age of eighty.

Through the years, acting began to overshadow Ethel's career as a singer. But true lovers of jazz and blues never deserted her. Actually, she always insisted that she really did not like to sing. "I do it for a living," she said. "I'd rather act." Ethel Waters did both with amazing talent and grace.

Mildred Bailey

Sweet and Pure

MILDRED BAILEY (1907–1951) of the sweet and pure voice brought in the era of the female big band singer. She joined the Paul Whiteman Orchestra in 1929, the first female singer who sang regularly with a jazz or pop orchestra. For more than two decades, she bridged the gap between jazz and swing. But many jazz fans know little about the timeless talent of Mildred Bailey. In part that is because she died at an early age and some of her early tunes were never recorded.

Mildred was short and overweight, an unlikely-looking figure onstage. Even more unlikely was the fragile tenderness of the voice that came from such a large woman. She did not look like a jazz singer, but she sang like one. And like the best of them, Mildred's work is timeless.

She was born Mildred Rinker in Tekoa, Washington, on February 27, 1907, but the family later moved to Spokane. Her father was Irish, her mother part Native American. Mildred got her musical start from her mother, a pianist who could play ragtime as well as classical music.

At the age of seventeen, Mildred worked in a local music store. She earned $10 a week singing the latest hits so that shoppers would buy the sheet music.

15

But in 1925, with an eye on a bigger career, Mildred took off for Southern California and Hollywood. By this time, she'd been married and divorced, although she kept her married name of Bailey. She was soon followed south by her older brother, Al, also a singer. Al brought along his longtime friend Harry Lillis Crosby, later known as Bing. Mildred helped them find jobs, and Crosby later credited her with starting his career.

Bandleader Paul Whiteman heard Mildred on a demonstration record and hired her in 1929. Within a year, she was earning $1,250 a week. Probably her greatest hit with the Whiteman band was composer Hoagy Carmichael's "Rockin' Chair" ("Ol' rockin' chair's got me, my cane by my side"). Soon, jazz fans were calling her the "Rockin' Chair Lady." Another great early hit was the classic and bluesy "Georgia on My Mind."

Jazz xylophonist Red Norvo joined the band in 1931, and Mildred married him in 1934. Two years later, they formed their own twelve-piece band with Mildred as the vocalist. They settled in New York City during the hectic Swing Era, becoming known as Mr. and Mrs. Swing. They also became known as the most fighting couple in the music business. Mildred had a classic temper, but Red matched her. They argued mainly in the recording studios, because Mildred made up her own mind about setting the tempo of a tune. The two divorced in 1945 but remained friends all their lives.

Throughout those years, Mildred Bailey made some classic recordings with such fine musicians as Johnny Hodges and Coleman Hawkins, Teddy Wilson, Benny Goodman, and the Dorsey brothers. Such tunes as the oh-so-easy "I've Got My Love to Keep Me Warm" and the sensitive styling of Duke Ellington's "I Let a Song Go Out of My Heart" display the fragile tenderness of Mildred Bailey's flutelike, extraordinary voice.

But in the late 1940s, when Mildred should have been at the top in the world of jazz and blues, her poor health sidelined her. Hindered by obesity all her life, she developed diabetes and heart trouble. In 1949, she went into semiretirement on a farm in upstate New York with her two dachshunds. She did emerge for occasional club engagements, but her health continued to fail. Mildred died penniless in a hospital in Poughkeepsie, New York, on December 12, 1951, at the age of forty-four. Longtime friends Bing Crosby and Frank Sinatra helped to pay her medical bills.

Never recognized as a superstar, Mildred Bailey is highly regarded by jazz experts. Her fellow musicians recognized her profound feeling for rhythm. Jazz lovers admire not only the lightness of her voice but also her magical touch with a lyric. She had a unique way of musically underlining the words as she sang them. A trait shared with Louis Armstrong was the knack of turning the most trite of lyrics into something just plain beautiful. It is a treat for the ear—the sweet, pure voice of jazz-stylist Mildred Bailey.

Mabel Mercer
Talking a Song

CAREER YEARS: 1930s–1980s

AT ONE POINT IN HER CAREER, critics complained that Mabel Mercer (1900–1984) "just can't sing." Mabel replied, "I know that. I'm just telling a story." Many, however, disagree with those critics. Frank Sinatra said Mabel Mercer taught him all he knew about singing. Johnny Mathis once told his audience to go hear Mabel down the block instead of asking him for an encore.

Mabel Mercer was an artist with her voice, a phraser of songs, a weaver of moods. In the St. Regis Room in New York City, where she performed for many years, she sat erect in a small armchair, her hands folded in her lap as she cast a spell with her precise storytelling set to music. For her ability to convey the emotional sense of a lyric, Mabel was studied by many of the great singers of her day, including Billie Holiday and Nat King Cole.

Mabel confessed that she was shy about singing and could not listen to her own music. Shy or not, she had almost no choice but to be in show business. She was born into a performing family on February 3, 1900, in Staffordshire, England. Her mother was a white vaudeville singer, her father an African-American who died before she was born. At school, she suffered the taunts of her classmates because of her mixed race. She remembered that it made her shy and a most self-conscious child.

But by age fourteen, Mabel had lost some of that self-consciousness when she joined the family's music hall act as a dancer. Her aunt, uncle, and cousins were part of a group called The Five Romanys, and Mabel toured with them. She enjoyed being part of the close-knit world of performers. By the time she was sixteen, she was a show business veteran and traveled with several other performing groups. Once she even joined a male quartet when the group lost a tenor and asked her to fill in.

After World War I, Mabel toured throughout Europe, including at the celebrated Bricktop's in Paris, where she first started to sing while seated on a chair. She said she got the idea because patrons at the café would call her over to their tables and ask for a tune. So she got used to singing while sitting down. Songwriter Cole Porter was one of the patrons at Bricktop's; he had a permanent table and became a great admirer of Mabel's. After he wrote a new song, he would often ask her to sing it; if it didn't sound right with Mabel's voice, it wouldn't sell elsewhere.

In 1938, Mabel Mercer married Kelsey Pharr, an American jazz musician, and came to New York City. Although the marriage did not last, Mabel's American career did. She first performed at Le Ruban Bleu and then spent several years at Tony's, a famous supper club on Fifty-second Street. But her soprano voice deepened, and she felt that she could no longer sing the notes as securely. So she began to talk the song in what is known as parlando, the art of talk-singing. That's when a critic said she couldn't sing, but music lovers adored her.

Although she rarely performed outside of New York City in the United States, Mabel had a great impact on many of the famous names in American music. People such as Barbara Cook, Peggy Lee, and Tony Bennett studied her style. And with her compelling talk-singing, she rescued many songs from obscurity, such as "While We're Young," "Little Girl Blue," and "Glad to Be Unhappy." Those tunes, along with "Fly Me to the Moon," became Mercer classics.

In the 1950s, Mabel bought a farm near Chatham, New York, where she lived with her dogs and cats and commuted to her singing engagements. For her seventy-fifth birthday, her admirers celebrated with a party at the St. Regis Hotel in New York City. A plaque marks the Mabel Mercer room.

The celebrated talker of songs received many honors for her work. She was given the Presidential Medal of Freedom by Ronald Reagan. She was the first recipient of *Stereo Review* magazine's Award of Merit, which was renamed the Mabel Mercer Award when it was given to Frank Sinatra in 1983. Mabel performed well into her eighties.

Mabel's years onstage ended in Pittsfield, Massachusetts, where she died of heart disease on April 20, 1984. For those who saw her in the cafés of New York and for those who hear her on numerous recordings, the voice of Mabel Mercer, the lady born to perform, is a rare and wonderful experience.

Billie Holiday

Matchless Lady Day

CAREER YEARS: 1930s–1950s

SO MANY ADJECTIVES have been heaped on Billie Holiday—*influential*, *original*, *extraordinary* among them. She truly was all that, but perhaps nothing captures the singer they called "Lady Day" so much as the word *matchless*. There was not before and there is not now any jazz singer quite like her. Some of her recordings from the 1930s are without equal in the history of jazz singing. Songs such as "I Wished on the Moon" or "What a Little Moonlight Can Do" illustrate her delicate, casual phrasing, her way of dragging the tempo while she kept on the beat. Billie Holiday changed the sound and the style of American popular music.

Billie rarely sang the blues; she *was* the blues. Every bit of heartache she endured in her short life was in her voice, especially when she sang "Mama may have, Papa may have, but God bless the child that's got his own." That was Billie in her magnificent loneliness, singing for her lost childhood. She wrote the lyrics of "God Bless the Child" about the poverty of her youth, and the song is forever associated with her.

She was known as Eleanora Fagan in Baltimore, Maryland, where she born on April 7, 1915. Her parents, Sadie Fagan and Clarence Holiday, married when she was three years old but soon divorced. Her father was a guitarist with some of the early jazz bands, and she later took his name. She also began calling herself Billie after the movie star Billie Dove.

Billie grew up poor and lonely, especially after her grandmother died. Her mother often left her with relatives who were abusive. When she was a young teenager, she scrubbed floors for food. At one of the places she cleaned, she heard a Louis Armstrong recording for the first time. His music crept into her heart and head and never left. On a rare visit to her father, he took her to a theater in Harlem where Armstrong was playing. She thought his "West End Blues" was the most beautiful song she had ever heard.

In 1928, Billie and her mother moved to New York City. Then came the Depression, and times got even tougher. They scraped by for a few years on what money her mother could make by cleaning houses. Eventually, Billie got so desperate for food that she went into a Harlem nightclub and asked for a job. She said she was a dancer. But after a short audition, it was obvious she could not dance. The owner asked if she could sing. The piano player started "Body and Soul," and Billie sang.

That was the beginning of the extraordinary career of Billie Holiday. A year or so later, John Hammond, a record producer for Columbia, heard her and recalled that she "sang with an exquisite sense of phrasing." Hammond organized recording sessions for her with some of the finest jazz musicians of the time. For the next seventeen years, Billie made some of the greatest jazz recordings ever. Her first recording (1933) was, however, somewhat less than memorable, even though the band included Benny Goodman and Jack Teagarden. The title was "Your Mother's Son-in-Law."

Besides recording, Billie joined road tours with Count Basie and Artie Shaw. The pay was bad, the hours on a bus monotonous and long. And for black entertainers traveling with a white band, the restrictions on eating and sleeping facilities were a nightmare. Billie never forgot the racism of those years.

She left the road tours for the nightclub circuit and soon became the most sought-after jazz performer in the city. At the beginning of this period, Billie recorded the unusual and painful "Strange Fruit," about brutal treatment of blacks in the South. It made her a star. Another recording that speaks of Billie's pain of racism is "Gloomy Sunday," a song of total despair. In addition, her series of recordings with a group led by pianist Teddy Wilson are some of the most beautiful in jazz history. Such tunes as "I Can't Give You Anything But Love" or "A Fine Romance" illustrate her ability to emphasize lyrics in her own relaxed style of phrasing. Some of her best recordings, however, date from 1937, when she teamed with friend and noted saxophonist Lester Young. When they met, the Harlem nightclub circuit referred to Billie as "Lady" because of the regal way she carried herself onstage. Lester added to the nickname by calling her "Lady Day," and it stuck. "Mean to Me" and "Foolin' Myself" are outstanding examples of their blend of voice and instrument.

But for all the fame and all the adoration, Billie never got over the sadness. Part of her was always that poor little girl in the black ghetto. The world was a mean, scary place. So Billie did what a lot of lonely and scared people do; she drank and she took drugs. She was arrested for a narcotics violation in 1947 and began the first of many fruitless tries to rid herself of the addiction. Still, she sang. She never stopped singing, and her fans never stopped loving her. However, because of her conviction, she was no longer allowed to appear in New York nightclubs. She performed in concert halls to constantly packed houses.

But finally the drugs took over. Her last performance was at New York's Phoenix Theater, where she had to be led off the stage after just two songs.

Billie Holiday died at the age of forty-four in a New York City hospital on July 17, 1959. The music world lost one of its most influential musicians, the matchless talent known as Lady Day.

Ella Fitzgerald

Simply the Best

THE MOST BELOVED JAZZ SINGER of the twentieth century, Ella Fitzgerald (1918–1996) was the lady with the easy, oh-so-perfect voice—simply the best. The winner of thirteen Grammy Awards, Ella had a three-octave vocal range and a style with such purity of tone that she could make her audiences laugh or cry on cue.

She was born in Newport News, Virginia, on April 25, 1918. The family, including her stepfather and half-sister, moved to Yonkers, New York, when Ella was quite young. She grew into an overweight youngster, as she would be an overweight adult. Despite that, she moved with amazing agility and grace onstage and on the dance floor. No one ever thought "fat" when Ella performed.

When Ella was sixteen, her mother died, and she began skipping school. She finally skipped school and home entirely for Harlem, where she danced for coins in the street. In 1934, she won an Amateur Night contest at the Apollo Theater. Chick Webb, a leading bandleader of swing at the time, heard about this young girl with the pure voice. He hired Ella in 1935. It was her version of an old nursery rhyme, "A-Tisket, A-Tasket" ("A brown-and-yellow basket"), that launched her to stardom.

When Webb died in 1939, Ella took over the band for two years while she continued to record. In the early 1940s, while touring with road shows, she began to experiment with "wordless" singing—known as scat. She explained it by saying that she just tried to do with her voice what the horns in the band were doing. In later years, there was no one who could scat quite like Ella.

Basically, scat singing is replacing the lyrics of a song with nonsense syllables and keeping the tune. But it is more than that. When singers scat, their voices become musical instruments. They are so in tune with the music that the listener is almost unaware that what he or she is hearing are not really words. It's the sound that becomes important. So it was with Ella.

Some of her last TV appearances were with Frank Sinatra. His way of scat singing was a kind of "do be do be do" tacked onto a line or at the end of a song. When they got together, Frank tried out his "do be do be dos" while Ella took off in a scat world of her own.

A change in Ella's career began in 1946 when she joined Jazz at the Philharmonic, led by Norman Granz. He produced Ella's Songbook albums, a long series of records featuring masters of American popular song such as Cole Porter and George Gershwin. During this period, Ella married bass player Ray Brown. They were divorced in 1953, and Ella never remarried.

Over the years, Ella became known for her pure tone and for her vocal inventions. She could send that girlish-sounding voice anywhere, skipping and sliding around her three-octave range. Some of her classic recordings are "Take the A Train," in which she sings Duke Ellington's little-known lyrics (the song is usually played as an instrumental); "Porgy and Bess" with Louis Armstrong; her unique "Mack the Knife"; and the hugely successful "Lullaby of Birdland."

Beginning in the mid-1950s, Ella began to receive numerous awards and honors as the first lady of jazz. She was on the cover of *Life* magazine. She got honorary doctorates from Princeton and Harvard. She took first place in the

Down Beat's Critics' Poll eighteen years in a row. In addition to her thirteen Grammys, this icon of jazz was given a Grammy Lifetime Achievement Award in 1967. In 1974, the University of Maryland began the Ella Fitzgerald School of Performing Arts. Ella accepted everything with her customary dignity and good grace, never quite seeming to believe that she was due all the praise.

Throughout the 1970s and 1980s, Ella toured with orchestras and played to ever-growing audiences. Her sweet silvery voice and vocal improvisations made her the most celebrated jazz singer—and the most loved—of her time. Most agreed with Bing Crosby and his statement years earlier: "Man, woman, or child, Ella's the greatest."

But in 1987, Ella underwent coronary bypass surgery, and her eyesight was failing due to cataracts. Her fans got used to seeing a serious-looking Ella Fitzgerald behind serious-looking spectacles. But she still kept performing to her considerably high standards. However, after having both legs amputated because of diabetes, Ella retired from the music world in 1993. She died on June 15, 1996, at her home in Beverly Hills, California, at the age of seventy-eight. She had the admiration of her peers and the love of millions of fans.

By the time of her death, Ella was long known as the First Lady of Song. But jazz fans have a shorter name for her. When they want to pick out the best, they just say "Ella." That is enough.

Anita O'Day
Swinging Style

CAREER YEARS: 1930s–Present

ONE EVENING IN AUGUST 2004, music lovers crowded the Iridium jazz club in New York City. They had come to hear the swinging style of a survivor—Anita O'Day. It is remarkable that they could hear her at all. Once the darling of the big band era, she has survived Depression-era walkathons, failed marriages, arrests and a jail term, heroin addiction, alcoholism, and a mental breakdown. Yet her unique style is still part of the appeal of this enduring jazz singer, now well into her eighties.

Anita never sang the way most singers do. At the age of seven when a doctor removed her tonsils, he accidentally snipped off a part of the soft palate. Because of that, she is unable to hold notes. When others sing "aaaaahhhh," Anita sings "ah-ah-ah." No matter how it sounds, it works for her.

It began working for her in Chicago, where she was born Anita Belle Colton on October 18, 1919. First she survived the endurance contests of the Depression era. In those so-called walkathons or danceathons, contestants tried to outlast one another on the dance floor for prize money. By the time she was nineteen, she was scratching out a living as a singing waitress. In the early 1940s, she graduated to local clubs and began using the stage name of

Anita O'Day. At one nightspot called the Off-Beat, she was heard by drummer and bandleader Gene Krupa. Anita joined Krupa and had several hits, including "Let Me Off Uptown" with trumpeter Roy Eldridge, who was the only African-American in the otherwise all-white band. But Anita and Eldridge fought all the time, and she developed a reputation for being moody and difficult.

Anita left Krupa for Stan Kenton and his band and by 1944 was ranked in *Down Beat* magazine. She was a great success, well on the way to a glorious career. Her performances were intense, her dry, husky voice slurring the melody as she handled a wide variety of songs. June Christy, Chris Connor, and others later picked up this husky singing style.

Some of Anita's greatest hits came in the mid-1950s with such songs as "You're the Top" ("you're the tower of Pisa, you're the top, you're the Mona Lisa") and "Honeysuckle Rose." Her 1956 recording of "Sweet Georgia Brown" was especially memorable as she starts in one tempo, in a duet with a drum, and switches tempos in midsong. With that tune and "Tea for Two," she brought down the house at the Newport Jazz Festival in 1958. Unfortunately, as Anita later admitted in her autobiography, *High Times, Hard Times*, she did not even remember performing at Newport because she was so high on heroin. And what should have been a career at the top began to slide. Her fast living brought on a mental breakdown. Her addiction brought on heart problems. In 1969, an overdose nearly killed her; in fact, she was declared dead, and then her heart started beating again. That trauma forced her to face what heroin was doing to her and her career. It took her a year, but she cured herself of the addiction. Anita O'Day has always been known as a tough-minded lady.

The tough-minded lady came back. Although she realized that the top of the charts would no longer belong to her, she built a niche as one of the best of the jazz singers. In 1985, she celebrated fifty years in show business with a performance at Carnegie Hall in New York City. Said the critics, "She still excels at up-temp rhythms." Anita performed with John Poole, her drummer for more than thirty years, and with Roy Eldridge, who joined her for the vocal duet they had created more than forty years earlier.

Besides singing at small nightclubs, Anita still does some tour work, often appearing with the famous guitarist Les Paul. She received a National Endowment for the Arts Jazz Masters Award in 1997. She calls herself a song stylist, not a singer. Anita O'Day is a wizard with jazz rhythms, easily controlling the timing of a song. But she speaks offhandedly of her talent, explaining her success as well as her survival with "It must be in the genes." For a lady who has outlived her traumas and still attracts jazz lovers, it must surely be much more than that.

Peggy Lee
All There Is

I'M A WOMAN, W-O-M-A-N," she half-sings, half-talks in her sultry voice. Then, in one of her hit recordings, she describes all the things she can accomplish. And that about sums up the life story of Norma Deloris Egstrom from Jamestown, North Dakota. In the field of jazz and pop there was, indeed, very little she could not do. Millions of fans know her as Peggy Lee (1920–2002), the tall blond with a whisper in her voice that went on and on.

It is hard to put Peggy Lee in a category. She was not just a jazz artist. Not just a pop artist. She was a small-town girl who became one of the most popular jazz singers and songwriters of the twentieth century. She was a thorough professional with fine phrasing and superb tone. She was a great diva with less than an octave-and-a-half range. She was a perfectionist, from her platinum hairdos to her expensive gowns to her dramatic entrances and exits. She was scandalous, tragic, and always colorful. In a world of music personalities filled with the unexpected, unusual, and unpredictable, she was one of a kind.

When Peggy Lee was too ill to attend a state dinner in the 1980s,

President Reagan sent her a telegram of good wishes. Peggy said, "The president of the United States. Can you imagine that? How did I ever get to here from North Dakota?"

Well, talent helps, and it showed up early. She was born on May 26, 1920, the sixth of seven children. Unhappy with an abusive stepmother and anxious to leave home, she began her singing career at age fourteen at the local radio station. Her next stop was the state capital of Fargo, where she earned $1.50 for a daily noontime show and changed her name to Peggy Lee.

From Fargo, she moved on to Chicago, where she sang in small nightclubs. She soon realized that audiences paid more attention when she was singing in a sort of whisper than when she belted out a song. Thus she developed an intimate style, rarely singing a note louder than needed. She also later changed the melodies and tempos totally as she saw fit. Peggy was heard by Benny Goodman and joined his band. Her rendition of the hard-times song "Why Don't You Do Right?" in 1943 sent her on the way.

Peggy married the band's guitarist Dave Barbour, the first of her four marriages. She and Barbour had one daughter, Nicki. At the time, she wanted to quit the band and settle down to married life, but Barbour thought she should not hide her voice. By the time Peggy left the Goodman band in 1943 to go solo, her career was assured. She became not only an accomplished musician but also a talented songwriter as well. She and Barbour had several hits, including "I Don't Know Enough About You" ("I know a little bit about a lot of things, but I don't know enough about you") and "Mañana," a 1948 tune that sold more than two million copies.

Peggy's career was in high gear in the 1950s. She branched out into film, playing an alcoholic singer in *Pete Kelly's Blues* (1955). Nominated for an Oscar, she lost out to Jo Van Fleet in *East of Eden*. Also in that year she wrote the lyrics and supplied several voices for the Disney animated film *Lady and the Tramp*. In 1958, Peggy sent the national temperature up a notch with her sultry recording of "Fever." It had been a hit rhythm-and-blues tune. Peggy kept the rhythm but added her own lyrics that pointed out the "very mad affair" between historical figures Captain John Smith and Pocahontas. Her recording hit number eight on the *Billboard* pop charts.

As the 1960s opened, Peggy Lee kept her music fresh by seeking out new talented musicians and songwriters. Two of Elvis Presley's writers came up with "I'm a Woman," her big hit in 1962. But if her career was flourishing, her health was not. She began a long battle with heart disease and diabetes. While singing at Basin Street East one night, she collapsed with double pneumonia. Left with permanent lung damage, she had to carry a huge oxygen tank as part of her traveling gear. She called it "Charlie" and used it two to four times a day to keep her lungs from filling with fluid.

In later years, Peggy was asked how she kept her career at the top for so long. She said she supposed she just kept up with the music. Through all the years, she adapted her music to fit the times, and it worked. Finally, after suffering a stroke, she died on January 21, 2002, at the age of eighty-one. She is the only female singer to have top-ten pop hits in the 1940s, 1950s, and 1960s.

Peggy Lee knew great success and heartache during her long years in the business. But she always seemed willing to take the next step, to try something new. Surely, there was another tune just around the corner. Amazingly, she did not receive her first Grammy until she was fifty, with the haunting "Is That All There Is?" about the subtle disappointments of life. One of the lines says: "If that's all there is, then let's keep on dancing, break out the booze and have a ball." For Peggy Lee, the song wasn't about sadness. It was about moving on, no matter what happens. And that's exactly what she did.

Dinah Washington

Gospel and Blues

CAREER YEARS: 1940s–1960s

"MISS D" HAD IT ALL—fame, wealth, adoration. Her admirers called her "The Queen," and she certainly lived like one. She wore splashy diamonds and exotic furs draped over her shoulders. She lived as though too much was never enough—jewelry, cars, alcohol, even husbands. She was married nine times.

But Dinah Washington (1924–1963) had something else, which made all the high living possible. She had a voice, a powerful instrument that some considered the best blues sound of the age. One critic described her singing as a "sharp but slightly jagged knife slicing through meringue." Her timing was masterly, her delivery impeccable. She often handled a lyric by half-singing, half-talking the words. She could be brash and erratic offstage, but in front of the microphone her flutelike voice was caressing and demanding. Called a giant in the 1960 *Encyclopedia of Jazz*, she has long been regarded as one of the finest blues stylists of all time. Unfortunately, Dinah's days in the spotlight were short; she died at age thirty-nine.

She was born Ruth Lee Jones in Tuscaloosa, Alabama, on August 29, 1924, but her parents moved to Chicago when she was three years old.

By the age of eleven, she was singing in the Baptist church choir. This tie to gospel music, combined with her gutsy blues style, eventually led to her unique delivery.

Dinah won an amateur singing contest at Chicago's Regal Theater when she was fifteen. After she began singing at the Garrick bar in 1942, she was overheard by Joe Glaser, head of a booking agency. He got her a job with Lionel Hampton's band. Hampton persuaded her to change her name, and Dinah stayed with the band until 1946. Two of her major successes with Hampton came in 1943 with her recordings of "Salty Papa Blues" and "Evil Gal Blues." By 1949, she was number one on the *Billboard* charts with "Baby, Get Lost."

During the mid to late 1950s, Dinah made some memorable recordings with the best musicians in the field and many duets with Louis Armstrong. "Blue Gardenia," featured in the 1955 jazz-based album called *Dinah Washington: For Those in Love*, is said to be one of her greatest ballads. She creates a rare mood and was compared to Billie Holiday. In addition to her voice, Dinah was an accomplished musician and could play several instruments. When she appeared at the 1958 Newport Jazz Festival, she "borrowed" one of the band vibraphones for a short rendition.

While her career was in high gear, so was Dinah's temperament offstage. She was a complex personality. And she knew how good she was. Dinah cared little about what she said to anyone and seemingly less about how she behaved. She entered a restaurant intending to shock people, and she often did. She once arrived at the famous Birdland club in New York with diamonds on the heels of her shoes. She appeared at a club in the South, where there had been a racial incident, with a pistol hidden in her fur stole. Dinah Washington lived life her way.

Eddie Chamblee, a tenor saxophonist who was Dinah's fifth husband, also saw a different side of her. Although her temper was fierce, he said she always apologized when she insulted people. And even though she fought constantly with her family, she always supported them financially.

In 1963, Dinah married her ninth husband, star defensive back for the Detroit

Lions, Dick "Night Train" Lane. In December, after being married only a few months, she took what was apparently an accidental overdose of sleeping and diet pills. She had just returned from a West Coast tour.

Dinah Washington left behind a vast library of recordings—blues, rhythm-and-blues, jazz, and pop tunes. No matter what the material, her voice reaches depths of emotion rarely touched by other singers. Whether it was Cole Porter's "Every Time We Say Goodbye" ("I die a little, every time we say goodbye, I wonder why a little") or Fats Waller's "Squeeze Me," it was all Dinah. She was brash, temperamental, difficult. But onstage and at her best, she was the incredibly talented "Miss D," eloquent, passionate, assured...and certainly unforgettable.

Sarah Vaughan

Pure Sass

S HE HAD A VOICE THAT COULD SLIDE from an operatic high note to a depth that made your toes wiggle. Sarah Vaughan (1924–1990) was one of the most glorious of all jazz singers. "Sassy" they called her. She was a fresh, sharp-tongued lady who left her audiences believing she meant each one of them when she sang "I get misty just holding your hand." When Sarah sang, love was beautiful and anything was possible.

Sarah Lois Vaughan was born in Newark, New Jersey, on March 27, 1924. She grew up with music. Her father was a carpenter who played the guitar, and her mother was a laundress who sang in the church choir. Sarah herself sang in the same choir by the age of seven. She was a soloist and played the church organ at age twelve. A few years later, she was spending so much time singing in local clubs that she dropped out of high school. Then in 1942, she won an amateur-night contest at Harlem's famous Apollo Theater. Singer Billy Eckstine, who was with the Earl Hines Orchestra, was in the audience. He told Earl to go hear the teenager. Earl's reaction was: "Is that child singing, or am I dreaming?" He offered her a job as singer and second piano in the band.

43

When Billy Eckstine left Earl to form his own group, Sarah went with him. So did star trumpeter Dizzy Gillespie and the great alto saxophonist Charlie "Bird" Parker. They were the pioneers of the bebop style, and Sarah developed an ear and a voice for its intricate harmonies and melodies. Whatever the guys could play on their musical instruments, Sarah could play on her voice.

Sarah began playing in New York City nightclubs in the late 1940s, where she met trumpeter George Treadwell, who became her manager and her husband. So began a decade of great recordings and worldwide tours. She joined Mercury Records in 1954 and produced her classic recordings of "Misty," "Tenderly," and a big commercial hit, "Broken Hearted Melody."

Sarah Vaughan used her voice as a live instrument. Her great range and effortless delivery combined with aching elegance. No matter what she sang, the lyrics came alive. "Look at me," she sang, "I'm as helpless as a kitten up a tree." The audience was charmed, and the mood was set for the romantic loveliness of "Misty."

In 1959, Sarah left Mercury to join Roulette Records, where she recorded some of her most outstanding work, especially with the Count Basie band, which is classic Sarah Vaughan. *The Divine One* album is an intimate setting, with tunes such as "You Stepped Out of a Dream" and "Have You Met Miss Jones?" In the 1960s, her partnership with Quincy Jones resulted in a number of memorable albums, most especially *You're Mine You*. She worked with Basie again in the 1970s, produced two Duke Ellington Songbooks, and introduced a hint of Latin music in her new arrangements.

Sarah was a somewhat eccentric performer. No matter how many concerts she gave, before each one she stood in the wings and declared that she simply could not go on. She always did. She also napped in her dressing room and liked to stay up for two or three nights in a row, attending parties or nightclubs.

Michael Tilson Thomas, a noted classical music conductor, asked Sarah to sing with the Los Angeles Philharmonic Orchestra honoring the music of George Gershwin. They later recorded the concert, and it is one of her finest works, winning her her first Grammy in 1981.

When it seemed as though the voice of Sarah Vaughan could only get better and better, the years of smoking caught up with her. While in New York City appearing at the Blue Note in 1989, she was diagnosed with lung cancer. She died on April 3, 1990.

There are great jazz artists, gifted jazz artists, even irreplaceable jazz artists. And besides those, there is Sarah Vaughan, in a class by herself, the sassy lady with the glorious voice.

as her stage name, Hampton began introducing her as Betty Bebop. He did not mean it as a compliment. However, in time, she dropped the Bebop and became Betty Carter.

Betty stayed with Hampton until 1951 when she decided to make it on her own in New York City. She began recording for Epic Records and appeared at such places as the Apollo Theater and the Village Vanguard as well as live concerts at the Newport Jazz Festival. In 1961 she recorded *Ray Charles and Betty Carter*, which became a classic. Featuring duets with the celebrated blind pianist, such as "Baby, It's Cold Outside" ("I really can't stay; but baby, it's cold outside; I've got to go away"), the album sent Betty to the top of the charts.

But the rest of the 1960s proved a hard time for Betty, as well as many other jazz artists. Soul music was "in," and pure jazz shifted to the background. So Betty formed her own recording company in 1969 called Bet Car. It was not a great commercial success, but she kept to her ideals of fresh jazz interpretations in a chamber music format. Even in a full concert, she always presented herself in a small instrumental ensemble of piano, drums, and bass, fairly unusual for a jazz vocalist. During this time, she was also raising two sons, Myles and Kagle Redding. Her marriage to James Redding ended in divorce.

Betty's career took an upswing in the 1980s when she signed with Verve Records. She won a Grammy in 1988 with her release of "Look What I Got!" And she also began to draw a huge following for her concert tours. Betty became recognized for her innovations in jazz singing and for her collaborations with well-trained musicians. In 1986 she was awarded the National Medal of Arts for her work. "The survival of jazz takes priority," she said.

Some critics commented on Betty's tendency to perform vocal tricks and gimmicks that obscured her supple voice. Without them, her voice showed its subtle shadings and appealing texture. She was a master of improvising. She was also a most able scat singer, the sounds delivered in a kind of machine-gun attack. Through the years her voice mellowed, becoming more vibrant, rich, and flexible. *Rolling Stone* magazine once noted that Betty Carter was totally devoted to jazz as an art form. She tried to make every performance new in the purist tradition of jazz. Both onstage and off, she was a forceful presence—earthy, even salty in her language, but always with true passion for her craft.

Then, suddenly, this innovative jazz vocalist was gone. She was diagnosed with pancreatic cancer and died at her Brooklyn, New York, home on September 26, 1998, at the age of sixty-eight.

Betty Carter is called one of the greatest pure jazz singers of the twentieth century. Demanding and uncompromising in her work, she constantly sought a new standard for her music. This did not always make her popular with promoters, and she gained a reputation as something of a prima donna because she took complete control of her concerts. But Betty knew what she wanted, and what she wanted was to keep people listening. "What do you do with a chorus and a half?" she once said. "You change things, stretch them out, change speed." For all of her professional life, Betty Carter changed things, always searching for that pure jazz sound…and very often coming very close.

Rosemary Clooney

Everybody's Singer

CAREER YEARS: 1940s–2002

ROSIE CLOONEY—one of television's biggest musical stars—thought of herself as a jazz-influenced pop singer. Indeed, she is best known for such hits as "Come On-a My House" and "White Christmas." But she counted among her musical influences Billie Holiday for her honest ability to show pain and Ethel Waters for her fine attention to lyrics. Rosie's rich, smooth, and deep voice caught the best of both styles, especially in her recordings on a small label, Concord Jazz, featuring the classics of Cole Porter, Duke Ellington, and others.

Rosemary was born in Maysville, Kentucky, on May 23, 1928, to an alcoholic father and a mother who traveled constantly on her job. When Rosie was thirteen, her mother left for California, taking Rosie's brother, Nick, with her. Her father, Rosie, and her sister, Betty, moved to Cincinnati. One night he went out to celebrate the end of World War II and never came back. The girls were on their own.

Collecting soda bottles bought an occasional meal but did not pay the rent. Then the girls won an open singing audition at a Cincinnati radio station, and the Clooney Sisters became an act. They sang on WLW for $20 a week—each. Their sound caught the ear of bandleader Tony Pastor, and they joined his orchestra in 1945. Betty returned to Cincinnati in 1948, but Rosie continued as Pastor's solo vocalist for another year. At age twenty-one, she headed for New York City, the hub of the music business.

Almost immediately, she got a recording contract with Columbia Records. There she met bandleader Mitch Miller, who convinced her to record a song with quirky lyrics called "Come On-a My House" ("Come on-a my house, my house-a come on"). She hated the song, but she sang it and won herself a gold record. The oddball tune made Rosemary Clooney a star.

Over the next decade, Rosie was indeed a star. She joined Bing Crosby's radio show. She appeared in a number of movies, notably *White Christmas*, the top moneymaker of 1954. Two years later, she had her own TV series, *The Rosemary Clooney Show*.

Rosie was on top of the world professionally but near the bottom of it otherwise. She married much-older actor José Ferrer in 1953, and the on-again-off-again union produced five children. In an attempt to keep it all together, she began to take sleeping pills and then drugs. She and Ferrer were divorced in 1961 but got back together and divorced again in 1967. This overall explosive situation got out of control after presidential candidate and friend Bobby Kennedy was assassinated in a Los Angeles hotel in 1968. Rosie was standing only a few yards away when it happened. The traumatic experience worsened her fragile mental health. Shortly afterward, she appeared at an engagement in Reno, Nevada, where she swore at the audience and raced off the stage. Then she was found driving on the wrong side of a mountain road in California and was admitted to a psychiatric ward. Her therapy continued for several years.

But Rosie was determined to make a comeback, which she did in 1976. Bing Crosby asked her to join him on his fiftieth anniversary tour. They sang "On a Slow Boat to China." She took another comeback step by signing the Concord Jazz contract, which resulted in a number of great hits for the rejuvenated singer. Fans who had thought of her as a pop singer warmed to her jazz recordings. Besides her new records, Rosie was highly popular at jazz clubs and in concert halls. She even won an Emmy nomination for her appearance on the popular TV series *ER*, joining her nephew, George Clooney, who was a member of the cast.

In 1996, the singer's comeback was enhanced by a number-one album, *Rosemary Clooney's White Christmas*. In that same year, she married an old friend, Dante DiPaolo. But in January 2002, during a routine physical, she was diagnosed with lung cancer. Rosie had been a longtime smoker. Part of her lung was removed at the Mayo Clinic in Rochester, Minnesota. That prevented her from being at the Grammy ceremonies, where she received a lifetime achievement award. Rosie Clooney died on June 29, 2002, at the age of seventy-four.

She was everybody's singer, a much-loved figure in the music world. She was mainly known as a talented interpreter of popular standards, but Rosie Clooney was a dedicated jazz singer, too. "I'll keep working as long as I live," she once said, "because singing has taken on the feeling of joy that I had when I started." The feeling of joy is what Rosie Clooney gave back to millions of music fans during a rocky but oh-so successful career.

53

Cassandra Wilson

Soulful and Sensual

CAREER YEARS: 1990s–Present

CASSANDRA WILSON ONCE CALLED JAZZ "a good old boys' club." She said few women "have been able to assert themselves as composers— not just as songwriters but composers—and bandleaders." Then she began to change things. Besides writing many of her own songs, in the late 1990s she was commissioned by Lincoln Center in New York City for six performances. She interpreted and produced the works of Miles Davis, the trumpeter and creative artist who died in 1991. Even so, she says, "the bias against women jazz singers is like racism—it doesn't go away."

This talented, outspoken artist is a wide-ranging performer. She can sound like Sarah Vaughan or her idol, Betty Carter. Her voice can be deep, dark, and seductive. She has a sparkling presence, her hair in long blond twists swinging as she bursts upon the stage. Cassandra is at home with jazz and blues, with pop, and with country and western. She can get deep into blues or torch songs and then delight audiences with her emotional version of Patsy Cline's great country hit "Crazy." Cassandra is simply at home on center stage.

She learned about center stage early on. Cassandra was born in Jackson, Mississippi, on December 4, 1955. Her father, Herman Fowlkes, an electric guitarist and high school music teacher, introduced her to music. When she was four, she sang at a school performance and embarrassed her parents because she was so loud.

Cassandra attended Jackson State University, where she studied communications, and was influenced by the gritty southwestern blues singer and composer Robert Johnson. But when she heard Betty Carter sing, she knew what her career would be. After graduation, she moved to New Orleans and then to New York City in 1983. At a jam session, she met saxophonist Steve Coleman, who encouraged her to write her own songs. The two made many recordings between 1985 and 1992.

Fans started to compare her to Betty Carter for her "I'll do it my way" attitude. Then Cassandra surprised them by recording an album of standards in 1988. Called *Blue Skies* ("Blue skies, smiling at me, nothing but blue skies do I see"), it was named *Billboard's* Jazz Album of the Year. That and her 1993 album *Blue Light 'Til Dawn* were turning points in her career. At first booked for concerts with headliners such as Miles Davis, she was soon a headliner herself. Besides her concerts and worldwide tours, she was chosen by trumpeter and composer Wynton Marsalis for a major role in his Pulitzer Prize—winning jazz opera, *Blood on the Fields*. It was recorded in 1997 and won her a Grammy nomination.

Some jazz critics question Cassandra Wilson's varied musical selections. Her reply is: "Hip-hop is jazz and so are the blues. They're interconnected; they're all part of a musical continuum. I don't live in a vacuum, and jazz doesn't exist in a vacuum either."

Most of Cassandra's publicity photos show a glamorous singer at work, with tousled hair and beautiful clothing. She doesn't mind being called glamorous, but she uses the word in a different sense. She speaks of being "glamoured," of being so connected with her music, of experiencing a feeling of being carried away. And at her concerts, she wants to share that feeling of "glamour" with her audiences. This sense of being connected drives her to experiment with different jazz forms.

In addition to singing, Cassandra plays the acoustic guitar. That may explain the close relationship she keeps onstage between her voice and the band instruments. Together the two present a mood, part of the "glamour" feeling. She says that her own understanding of music has enabled her to talk to musicians who perform with her. She can talk to them about chord changes, for instance. That allows her to have a degree of closeness and harmony with other musicians that is not always achieved by other singers. She admits that she is very involved in technique when she is writing music or practicing for a concert. But when the technique is done, the performance turns to pure emotion.

Cassandra Wilson is gaining the attention of the jazz world not only for her compelling voice but also for her willingness to experiment with all aspects of her field. Whether she is scat singing or pouring her heart into "Amazing Grace," Cassandra is one with her music, an important, innovative, still-growing figure in the jazz world of the twenty-first century.

Diana Krall

In the Classic Mode

CAREER YEARS: 1990s—Present

A T A **1999** JAZZ CONCERT IN CARNEGIE HALL, the entire audience seemed to hold its collective breath for a moment. That was when Diana Krall, a fine pianist with a thoughtful mastery of harmonies, turned from the keyboard to sing "When I Look in Your Eyes." This low-key diva has a husky, seductive contralto voice and an uncanny ability to tell a story in her songs. She creates an intimate relationship between her voice and the piano, and it stops an audience cold. Without gimmicks, she is a quietly captivating, impressive talent not yet at the top of her career.

Working toward that career began in Nanaimo, British Columbia, Canada, where Diana was born into a musical family on November 16, 1964. She played the piano as a youngster and won a scholarship to Boston's famed Berklee College of Music, where she studied for eighteen months.

Diana returned home and attended a jazz camp in the state of Washington in 1983. There she met master bassist Ray Brown Jr., who urged her to go to Los Angeles for more study. He was convinced she had a career in jazz. Diana recalls that her mother was not so sure.

However, she did move to Los Angeles, where she studied with Jimmy Rowles, pianist for such singers as Billie Holiday and Peggy Lee. He also encouraged her to develop her sultry voice. She began performing in L.A. piano bars, then moved to Toronto, and finally to New York City in 1990. Three years later she recorded her first album, *Stepping Out*, with bassist John Clayton and Jeff Hamilton on drums. That got her a recording contract with the GRP label, and Diana stepped out into the world of jazz.

Diana's second album, in 1996, was called *All for You*, a tribute to the great Nat King Cole. Like Cole, she demonstrates her ability to weave a story and mood into her singing. A highlight of the album is the novelty tune "Frim Fram Sauce," recorded by Cole in 1945 ("I want the frim fram sauce with the ausen fay, with chafafa on the side"). The album won a Grammy nomination and headed the U.S. jazz charts for more than two years.

During the 1990s, Diana Krall went from little-known pianist to jazz glamour girl. She catches the eye even before she catches the ear. An attractive, tall, green-eyed blond, she is uncomfortable with the glamour image and confesses to being somewhat shy. But she is learning to live with the growing pressure of being in the musical limelight.

Diana's career really skyrocketed in 1998 with her hit single, a Fats Waller tune called "Peel Me a Grape." This jazz standard was virtually owned for years by wispy-voiced Blossom Dearie, but Diana delivers the witty tune in a model of wise understatement.

Diana makes her home in New York City and frequently visits her family in Canada. In December 2003, she married pop-punk pioneer Elvis Costello in a ceremony performed at Elton John's castle in London. She and Elvis cowrote six songs for her eighth album, *The Girl in the Other Room*. In 2004 she was named international musician of the year at the National Jazz Awards.

With her career growing as quickly as her fan base, Diana is on a very fast track to stardom. She is a commanding performer, relaxed and yet intimate with an audience. She remains modest about her success and low-key about the jazz world's attention. Call her sultry, call her the toast of the new jazz scene. But of all the praise she has received, she is probably most pleased with this comment by the *New York Times*: Diana Krall is "a superb jazz pianist and an even better singer."

Bibliography and Further Reading

Albertson, Chris. *Bessie*. New York: Stein and Day, 1972.

Balliett, Whitney. *American Singers*. New York: Oxford University Press, 1988.

Bauer, William R. *Open the Door: The Life and Music of Betty Carter*. University of Michigan Press, 2003.

Cheney, Margaret, and Rex Reed. *Midnight at Mabel's: The Mabel Mercer Story*. Washington, D.C.: New Voyage Publishing, 2000.

Chilton, John. *Billie's Blues*. New York: Stein and Day, 1975.

Clarke, Donald. *Wishing on the Moon: The Life and Times of Billie Holiday*. New York: Viking, 1994. Reprinted in paperback, Da Capo Press, 2002.

Clooney, Rosemary, with Joan Barthel. *Girl Singer: An Autobiography*. New York: Doubleday and Company, 1999.

Clooney, Rosemary, with Raymond Strait. *This for Remembrance*. Playboy Press, 1977.

Crowther, Bruce, and Mike Pinfold. *Singing Jazz*. San Francisco: Miller Freeman Books, 1997.

Friedwald, Will. *Jazz Singing: America's Great Voices from Bessie Smith to Bebop and Beyond*. New York: Charles Scribner's Sons, 1990; New York: Da Capo Press, 1996.

Gourse, Leslie. *Louis' Children: American Jazz Singers*. New York: William Morrow, 1984; New York: Cooper Square Press, 2000.

———. *Sassy: The Life of Sarah Vaughan*. New York: Charles Scribner's Sons, 1993; New York: Da Capo Press, 1994.

Haskins, James. *Ella Fitzgerald: A Life Through Jazz*. London: New English Library, 1991.

———. *Mabel Mercer*. New York: Atheneum, 1987; New York: Welcome Rain Publishers, 2002.

———. *Queen of the Blues: A Biography of Dinah Washington*. New York: William Morrow, 1987.

Holiday, Billie, with Dufty, William. *Lady Sings the Blues*. Garden City, Long Island: Doubleday and Co., 1956; New York: Avon Books, 1956; New York: Penguin Books, 1984 and 1992.

Kliment, Bud. *Ella Fitzgerald, Singer*. New York: Chelsea House, 1988.

Lee, Peggy. *Miss Peggy Lee*. New York: Donald I. Fine, 1989.

Nicholson, Stuart. *Ella Fitzgerald.* London: Victor Gollancz 1995; Boston: Northeastern University Press, 1995.

O'Day, Anita, and George Eells. *High Times, Hard Times.* New York: G. P. Putnam's Sons, 1981; Limelight Editions, 1988.

O'Meally, Robert. *Lady Day: The Many Faces of Billie Holiday.* New York: Arcade Publishing, 1991; New York: Da Capo Press, 2000.

Pleasants, Henry. *The Great American Popular Singers.* New York: Simon & Schuster, 1974.

Waters, Ethel. *His Eye Is on the Sparrow.* Garden City, Long Island: Doubleday and Company, 1951; Westport, Conn.: Greenwood Press, 1978; New York: Da Capo Press, 1992.

Discography

The following compact discs contain at least a few of the best-known songs of each of the artists. All of them are reissues. In alphabetical order by artist, the CDs recommended at this time are:

Mildred Bailey. *The Rockin' Chair Lady*, Verve, 1994; includes "Rockin' Chair" and "Georgia on My Mind," two of her biggest hits.

Betty Carter. *Inside Betty Carter*, Blue Note, 1993; includes "My Favorite Things" and "Open the Door." These songs demonstrate the versatility of the singer.

Rosemary Clooney. *16 Biggest Hits*, Sony, 2000; includes "Mambo Italiano," "Botch-a-Me," "Come On-a My House." Though these songs were not the best songs in her repertoire, they helped make her a household name, and then she went on to record some of the most important songs by leading composers in American popular music.

Ella Fitzgerald. In *The Diva Series*, Verve, 2003; includes "Mack the Knife" and "How High the Moon."

Billie Holiday. In *The Diva Series*, Verve, 2003; includes "Don't Explain," "Billie's Blues," "God Bless the Child," "What a Little Moonlight Can Do," from among her best-loved hits.

Diana Krall. *When I Look in Your Eyes*, GRP, 1999, her first Grammy winner; *Live in Paris*, Universal, 2002; includes "The Look of Love" and "Devil May Care." Krall received a Grammy Award for this album.

Peggy Lee. *The Best of the Singles Collection*, Capitol, 2003; includes "Fever" and "Is That All There Is?"

Mabel Mercer. *Sings Cole Porter*, Rhino Records, 1994. Miss Mercer was noted for her great interpretations of Porter's songs. Another album showing off her artistry as an interpreter of songs is *The Art of Mabel Mercer*, Collectibles, 2001; includes "While We're Young."

Anita O'Day. In *The Diva Series*, Verve, 2003; includes "Tea for Two." Her interpretation of this song, which was filmed during a Newport Jazz Festival in 1958, became legendary.

Bessie Smith. *The Collection*, Sony, 1989; includes "Down Hearted Blues."

Sarah Vaughan. *Ken Burns Jazz*, Polygram, 2000; includes "Send in the Clowns," one of her trademark songs, which she sang at nearly every performance late in her life, and "If You Could See Me Now," a major hit from her early recording career.

Dinah Washington. *What a Diff'rence a Day Makes!* Universal, 2003; includes the title song.

Ethel Waters. *The Incomparable Ethel Waters*, Sony, 2003; includes "Stormy Weather" and "Heat Wave," two of her best-known songs.

Cassandra Wilson. *Blue Skies*, Polygram, 1990; includes "Polka Dots and Moonbeams" and "Blue Skies."

64

Note: Because Louis Armstrong was so influential for the early singers such as Billie Holiday, here is a representative CD: *The Best of Louis Armstrong: The Hot Five and Seven Recordings*, Sony, 2002. This includes a quintessential jazz-singing recording, "West End Blues," from 1928.

Special thanks to Andrea Natta, an employee of Barnes & Noble in the music store on Sixth Avenue at Twenty-second Street, New York City, for her help in compiling this list of currently available releases.